M000307773

MINE

▽

TUNG-HUI HU

*To Jerry
with best
wishes
Tung-Hui Hu*

53

AUSABLE PRESS
2007

Cover art: "Rosendale" by Jill Moser
1997. Casein and ink on USGS map
27" x 22" Courtesy of the artist

Design and composition by Ausable Press
The type is Bembo.
Cover design by Rebecca Soderholm
Author photo by Andrew Moisey

Published by
Ausable Press
1026 Hurricane Road
Keene, NY 12942
www.ausablepress.org

Distributed to the trade by
Consortium Book Sales & Distribution
1045 Westgate Drive
Saint Paul, MN 55114-1065
(651) 221-9035
(651) 221-0124 (fax)
(800) 283-3572 (orders)

The acknowledgments appear on page 65 and constititute a
continuation of the copyright page.

© 2007 by Tung-Hui Hu
All rights reserved
Manufactured in the United States of America
First Edition

Library of Congress Cataloging-in-Publication Data

Hu, Tung-Hui, 1978—
Mine / Tung-Hui Hu. –1st ed.
p. cm.
ISBN-13: 978-1-931337-33-5 (alk. paper)
I. Title.

PS3608.U22M56 2006
811'.6–dc22
2006031681

ALSO BY TUNG-HUI HU

The Book of Motion (2003)

MINE

BALANCE

Soon after I moved to California
I felt tremors everywhere. It made for
headaches and a vivid idea of how
delicately each thing was balanced,
bird upon sky, sky upon roof, roof
upon post & lintel. What trees I saw
had shifted in their sockets towards the
sky, some hanging loose and some
undressed by fire until black, wire-tipped,
and deaf. The heat loosened from
the ruptured earth was the same heat
I felt once leaving the surgery room—
with one eye cut I saw things as a
fish does. A flat world, pulled
in all directions by this tremendous
current that sets down the world's
balance, aligns people with doors
and throws me off the sidewalk,
a tremor of mind: in less than a small
touch I crumple down, and the tea
I am holding is immersed in the
puddles, and my body turns
the waters fragrant.

POTTER'S FIELDS

A pot found while digging
slipped out of the soil as
a fish is deboned. God is said
to have formed man as easily,
moulding him from dirt as on
a potter's wheel, but what men
could you find crossing the borax
flats that shine whitely, the air
thick with salt and residue of rare
earth metals upwelled from the crust,
occasional ships from the earlier
half of this century gutted,
splayed, the sound of the motorbikes
rattling the moorings, a sea transposed
from wetness, distilled, a sea
meaning masts, pots, bones.

LISBOA 1755

The day the earthquake came capsizing even the battleships in the bay I was watching João Manuel de Lourenço fashion a ring out of some inscrutable alloy he had fished out with a gleam in his eyes and which I secretly named adamantite. This ring I was to use to court Isabel Amorim and that she would resist my advances a fifth time was unfathomable: on this point my jeweler assented wholly. For he could feel each mineral as an organ swelling inside the earth and as we spoke had even begun to taste the metal, biting the gold as if he could feel its softness. Consequently the links and chains he fashioned were not to bind the neck or the ankle but for the sadness and melancholy that one carries like a worn passport. But even as he worked I heard the bells of the church outside give a terrible groan and burst, and I thought Senhor de Lourenço had fallen off his chair, only it was the earth that gave way, the drawers splaying open to reveal a strange light of metals. And as he fumbled around on the floor as an overturned tortoise flails its legs it was then I realized the man was blind, this man whom I had grown to trust better than my own hands.

NOT THAT OUR EMPIRE DECLINES

Do you know the woman who grinds
a pestle of iron year after year against
the rocks? Her eyes are closed, thinking
of all the things that need repair:
the buttons come off shirts,
the fish in the oceans. The truth is,
civil servants are here to staunch

the decay, not that our empire declines
but that it has grown like fruit trees
planted in flower pots.
The graft will not
take here, so repair the rootstock,

repair the spine tissue that keeps her awake
at night, repair the burn mark from father,
repair the cat which speaks as it
reaches up for meat on the shelf,
repair to the dining room,
repair the cow jumped over the moon

and the sheep come crashing down
onto the fence, repair that too.

ABOUT DIRT

To plunge your hand into dirt
is to say, come here, I want to kiss you,
but to sift it between your fingers
is poverty, each clump sticking
like grains not scraped
from the side of a bowl.

Good dirt, bad dirt.
These canyons a crowded market,
everyone with something to tell you,
no one listening back. Go on, wet it,

put a ball into your mouth: the sun
which has been lost in the mountains

will come out and while still ductile
soft hands will shape you into
lizards and tree-roots.

THE STRIKE

We set out for the mountains
since they had not been crippled
by the strike, people moving across
roadsides, chatting to neighbors.
For not lifting carrots out of fields,
was the government against us? No,
the government was on strike as well,
our prince opened his knapsack of
cheese and grapes to offer us a slice,
his announcer out with laryngitis
for the day. From across the sea
rumors came that other countries
were furious, that we had violated
our own sovereignty, that we should
be declassified as a principality,
their boats nudging prow to prow, bay
water flowing thickly between their
oars, and the city emptied, the plazas
empty, the only signs to direct
the invaders: "men, women."

TELEGONUS, LATINUS, AGRIUS

They set up camp briskly as generals
gathering in the plains. After the bellboy
turns away she unbuttons her cuffs
and he begins to unwind the dressing on her
arm, motioning for her to turn this way
or that, fanning the wound turned
whitish, and she thinks of how
she once brought milk
to a picnic with a lover, but it had curdled,
and poured out in lumps.

When she goes outside in the rain
the word *affair* is still harsh in his ears.
He tells himself this is no less real
than the three sons they will produce,
the relief he feels at her absence, or the green
apple that he has left for her balanced
against her black skirt.

THE GRACEFUL COUNTRY

It was easy to say what our country wanted fifty years ago: to be beautiful and graceful, like the time a man had landed on the moon, and everyone was listening on the radio. That silver ship moving through the air. That way of entering a room. Now we are a well-mannered country, but we cannot suddenly speak roughly any more than golf courses can be turned back into sand pits. We want to smell like iodine and cheap perfume again. Over there, by the boardwalk: the same strip of land where we once slept, our backs to the sea, fires at our ships.

INSTRUCTIONS RECEIVED
BY NEW COLONY

One soldier's rifle at my back:
for a minute we walked
like this, his barrel, my shirt,
I leading the way, a brother
showing a brother where
to eat, where to hide. Nothing
was wrong the night of Easter,
only this bell calling us
down from the hillside,
its throat saying metal-for-
heartbeats, rise-and-fall-of-the-day,
hope is lost, war is won, orange
trees and candlewax burning.

Here is what the soldier thought:
the footraces when we were young—
people would slow down to scoop
up the yellow apples we would
toss, crisp as a bell ringing.
No, it was more like this:
after the hunt the air is
heavy with birds and frogs,
their lungs inflating like a bell
set loose in the ocean.

*

Go, then, to the place where they still sew with
needles of boar bristle, and build your
city there. How boars are caught:
in the trees, some men chase, others run,
imitating pheasants.

★

You were burned once by their rope
that sang like a bird. You clung to it
like a boy holding a blade of grass.

Now they give you mud walls and spaces
between rocks, arms of trees outstretched
to point the way skywards, weeds and weeds
for health. They give you cities of
ladders and ramparts. When you see

a woman appear you stay there,
this woman (Kore you call her) of rope
that is to say with feet tied together
you bury her.

★

Not that way.

*

Like you, I hated running
from country to country, each
place the same people, just
uglier, older, as if a
gigantic hand had pressed hard
against their faces, fusing
together bones, leaving some
cross-eyed, color-blind. And yet
in the plains we can feel
the lake rising at our backs,
steamships that cross when fog sets
over the cornstalks, the sight
of pumpkins and squash splayed
on vines like exposed ovaries,
bumps and all, orange, green.
When our neighbor gave us zucchini,
we tried for a week to get rid
of it, zucchini in bread,
zucchini in applesauce,
zucchini in pies, and what
we think he was saying was
simple: Vines, not people,
follow you everywhere you go.

THE WISH ANSWERED

Several years ago I discovered
how easily love and food are confused,
when I thought I was in love with someone
but really it was a skipped lunch,
forgive me, I was young,
passions being what they were
were somewhat equivalent, mixed-up,
the highest anything,
stars without firmament, colors huddled
in the back shelf of a dark closet.
And even when I got my wish,
her sitting in front of me,
all I could think about
was cannoli, biscotti.
How embarrassing! My stomach
growled and my heart leapt.

FIVE DOLLARS

She tells you to bring her five dollars. You go home.
You look for change in the couch. You bring it to
her. She turns off the light. You lie in the dark with
your clothes off. Nobody moves. You have seen geese
stunned after flying into a glass window: it is the same
thing with your bodies. You hope something will
change color. You hope it is something uprooted in-
side of you. You start to worry someone will find you
still there the next morning. Your neck is beginning to
get sore. You say Is that it? She says Yeah, that's what it
is. The lights go on. You look down. It is the dew that
appears after a summer night.

SCHOOL OF DENTISTRY

They go to the shore
to eat grapefruit. She lances
the peel with her thumbnail
and they bite into it, bursting
nodes and translucent
clusters inside. Even after they
drive home he can still feel
the dampness on his neck,
in his eyes. He presses each spot
that marks him like stigmata
reminding him of low
tide and rocks glistening
in the fog as if he were probing
with every step the mouth of
some creature greater than he.
He knows that plovers clean
meat from the teeth of
crocodiles,[1] but to descend
into the darkness, a wet unseeing
that engulfs him like a cave
studded with cabochons:
it is a motion he has feared since
a small child, before he knew of
things like plovers, vaginas,
grapefruit.

[1] So says Herodotus, but G. L. MacLean (1996) writes
that "no reliable observer since then has seen [the plover]

acting as a crocodile toothpick... The myth has been perpetuated in the literature and needs finally to be laid to rest, unless contrary proof can be found." From *Family Glareolidae* (Coursers and Pratincoles) pp. 364-383 in del Hoyo, J., Elliott, A., & Sargatal, J., eds. *Handbook of the Birds of the World* vol. 3. Lynx Edicions: Barcelona.

SCHOOL OF TAXIDERMY

Listen, see that boy who discovers
a dead squirrel at the foot of the tree,
he thinks it is worth something,
he thinks he will skin it and they
will have a fair and sell it. And he
tells his friend and his friend is
excited, too. Then night falls and
they return to fetch the broken
corpse which is encrusted like
a jewel with moss or a cake with
crumbs, the maggots white,
swarming, churning away
the squirrel's eyes. And he does
not know how to rid himself
of it now that he has it.

That boy is me I was that boy

HIKING TO SUGARLOAF

My father once carried me
on his shoulders to the old
whiskey still past the canal
and up the mountains, which
was different from his grasp
on my leg as he swung me
in anger before reaching for
the belt. The smell of aniline
leather, tannin from rainwater
left in a stump, sting of a
first sip of spirits, fall
leaves spinning as if a child's
mobile hanging in a bedroom:
whether I held onto him or
he held onto me, both had
the same touch, which we
discuss rarely these days,
now it is my hand on his
stomach, which is softer now,
folds in on itself. Is sightless.

MISREADING SOLOMON

When you walk through doorways,
I am aroused by the way you divide the
world into two equal pieces.
Easy as opening cantaloupe.
You have just learned to toss your hair
back so I will give you
a bar of rosin to give it shape
and the horsehair bow inherited
from grandmother. I think of your hands
moving like the cavalry in the Crimean
war and how a soldier would carry
a flask of cognac by his side.
I think of your height, since only
now, sitting, our faces line up,
bone to bone. I think of your height.
If you are a wall I will build
a tower of silver on you.

SCHOOL OF ARCHITECTURE

Walking outside was strictly forbidden. So was running, crawling, swimming, and all the other motions we devised to get around this rule: the circumflex, the hand-skip, the foxtrot. Yet how were we to run errands or visit our friends who knew nothing of our situation and offered no sympathy? We had no choice but to extend the lines, first with boxes and tunnels, then, as we got older, divots of steel and plexiglas. Out from our house warbled limbs, fragile limbs that snapped in and out of being, cradling us wherever we went.

SAIGNÉE

They chew on flowers to bring color
back to their faces. Inside the rows of
bougainvillea they eat the purple and the
ochre that climb up the walls, and I want
to say I too know the solitude that divides
blood into bright cell and plasma
that leaves a fluid pale as the eye of a partridge.
I too know no cure for it except to keep eating.

At dawn sunlight stains the city the blush
of onion-skin and the muezzin's voice
rings out over the rooftops. He is the foghorn
that pierces the heart before morning,
rising from the ocean's octaves to burn off
the clouds, and yet it terrifies me, to think
early some day you will wake up to see me

standing by the balcony as if I and my legs
and my robe were part of the railing,
you will put your arms around me and ask
why I stand there and I will have no answer.
You do not stir, but I know you have seen
men tumble out of the sky, and with
every ululation your body trembles in sleep.
Though we lie next to each other we are
in different countries, one with water,
one without.

SULFUR

They are setting fire to the field
and as the work day has started
slowly we go out to watch
the sky yellowing like sulfur.
I know they are burning leaves
off sugarcane in the distance,
thousands of cut stalks lying across
furrows, a pyre that leaves a smell
sour as manure, but in the bone-
cavities the sap keeps moving.

She tells me that as a girl she
used to run through the yard
before she knew what nakedness
could mean. She would like to
do that again, though there are
more clothes now. She would
like to take my hand and run
hissing through the brush and
rub her hands in the smoke.
She could always run, and if
I were younger I would follow.

EARLY WINTER, AFTER SAPPHO

Some say the air of
early winter moving through
windows. For some, black ships

coming towards the city
are the quietest sounds on earth.
But I say it is with whomever one loves.

And very easily proved:
when we are trying to think of
something to say to each other,

each remembering back
who said what, the ground
we've already covered,

you can hear all the money
lost earlier in the stock market,
even fresh water slipping
into salt water.

HOW TO CARE?

That month, I wondered where they gathered
before hospitals, before the oncology ward,
intensive care, urgent care.

Back then it was all urgent, binding
hands and feet, immobilizing the body
before it could pass into cadaver. Now
it is easier, to look at photographs instead,

one of him in his work shirt, collar fraying,
stretched across his ribs. Another, his daughter,
who sets his shaven head upon a pillow as if
arranging flowers. Practice for the living,

walking through hallways, reading charts,
X-rays, seeing the hollows of a torso held
to the light, getting juice from the cafeteria,
swallowing it, passing it out of me,

it was like being on an ocean liner, the same
slowness to move, the same distance from land,
where men are hurting, men are living.

ON POWER OUTAGES

Knowing someone by touch is like being able to move around a dark city without power or signs. And even when it is easy to move around it is always awful to be inside. One man proposed during the blackout, it was reported on the news. Another is inside, sitting quietly—everybody can hear him thinking to himself, trying not to move, waiting for the morning to rise.

She tells him to wait and she will send somebody to fix the heat. She slips a coat over him and leaves the door unlocked and leaves him tapping stiffly at the countertop, which is stone, polished blackness, all faults and grain and stars in it rubbed out. The dark of the city like an oil seep, and he says Home once brought shelter, end of night. He taps to himself. One mississippi, two mississippi.

PASSAGE INTERDIT AUX
NON MUSULMANS

For you they come down from the mountains
bearing oranges and dates to this sweetest
of places. In the dust where donkeys pull

carts of mint leaves wet dirt and clay
men surround you and demand to know your name
and will not let you leave. To discover you stand
on someone else's land whose blood has made
these walls of *pisé*[1] and cactus that encircle you

who try to find a passage through his city the red
city which you cannot enter except by deception.
Do words exist only to drive men apart? You talk of a
desert plant named mimosa that folds up into itself

when burnt or touched and what you still smell
is the sweetness of mimosa in the heat.

[1] – *pisé, pisé de terre* (French 'pounded earth') *The Thames & Hudson Dictionary of Art Terms*

STORY OF MAN'S DESIRE

They say the night watchman
is so good he can hear
the grass growing and when he
puts his ear to the ground
it's all the sounds pleasurable
to you, a boy and girl
coupling at dawn while your
bed lies empty, the grain
elevators lifting winter wheat
already sprouting into the air,
sound of hot water rising
in a dark room as you cup it
waiting for the movies to start,
sound of sodium lamps across
asphalt like the wingbeats
of a bird held in your hand.
You think he listens because
he's working on a book he'll
call "Story of Man's Desire."
Inside, a thousand identical
ink drawings of the night sky
as we move across it: on paper
we make cubes, crystals,
even the slipping in and out
of sight a type of crystal.

AND ABOUT TIME

I

"While you were away
I sent for Moira to come and rub
away the crookedness in souls
that does sometimes slip out from
view like crowbars or amphorae

that you call your dark side
because you do not wear
it well (call it a crooked smile on your face)

and the silence that hung catenary
over the ending chord in the song
I used to play as a child—that too ended

and rain fell turning lawns
the vitreous color of eyes"
the voice said (it was mine).

2

Though we had known each other for months, this is how we first met. I was crossing a stone bridge when she wrapped herself around me. I followed her inside a building where pieces of marble broke from the steps under the treading of my feet. Look at the lines she said. See how old they are. The veins in the floor—quartz, I think—streamed away like a wrist and I felt like I was walking on a living thing: this is the effect she had on me.

3

I'm speechless I don't know what
to say she said. We are a very good company
and I'm sorry you feel this way about us
she said. Let me tell you

about getting lost about halfway up
the mountainside: we needed

water but none of it was clean.
It was maybe getting giardia or heat
exhaustion and so we drank. So too
the argument one-sided as it was

and a few months later
we will remember the other
by thinking Oh! Where did the time go?

4

In purity you have removed everything
from your room & as a canyon holds a bridge
in its arms your body stretches
across morning. With eyes
closed or open it is the same,
sheets and walls and summer sky.
Soon you will smell the cigar
smoke from the courtyard so that
even the palm leaves are dripping

in it, you will walk
to the sink to wash your hands
of the blood you have accumulated
igneous as basalt. And you will say
to us I am so beautiful I am
the meridian between the days.

5

Now wake up before the birds awake and fly to
another city to work until nighttime. Sleep here
sweating under the afternoon ceiling fan.
Thank these persons for nothing accomplished and
drive an hour for a glass of aqua vitae. These
months I loved more than anything else—incandescent, I blazed
like a hoarse voice, like gas-lamps,
like traffic lights beneath a rainy day.

6

There are three notes in this song I can stand
and the rest just scaffolding like the white

moat that surrounds a wound.
Listen, here are the things I will not

speak to you about because then I'd have nothing left:

a maple bench, smooth to the touch. Glenn Gould singing
in the background of his recordings.
The ability to jerk your hand
out of harm's

way: say from a hot stove. And slats of light
through the shutters.

7

When we are very rich (so rich that
the gilt on sunlight belongs to us) we will
say to ourselves: "And about time." And
there will have been no gap between

when we first desired and when we got.
So this is to fill in all those
moments in between,
those you will have no memory of—

once when everything was wrong
you (stronger than daybreak) tore
apart the living room. Splinters
and plant soil on the floor.

And when it was over
you arose, thinking There will be hell to pay.

Nobody said a thing
and this knowledge has hurt you
more than anything else.

SCHOOL OF RHETORIC

Every seven years there are cicadas,
just like that: the year I beat up
the preacher's son, the year I fell in
love. The air gets rich with the sounds
of their wingbeats. Imagine your skull
cavity resonating like a pipe organ with
their mating-calls every second of
the day. People get irrational. Perhaps
that explains everything I did. There is
nothing else you can do, while you are
stepping over these bodies of insects
that explode like oranges thrown at
asphalt, when the ground becomes
liquid with cicada shells, except beat
people up or fall in love.[1]

[1] – This is a lie.

A SEASON OF COAL

Even if shoes stick to the road
and coal seams break
the surface, this is a nice place
to live. Quiet. Warm.

So the black
earth has failed you;
still there are wide streets,
trimmed grass,

plenty of coal
carried by thieves
as a symbol of protection.

Or to turn people
monochrome. To coal another:
fingers pulled like cloth

over a birdcage
cover the eyes and vanish
the anger. As if in the dark
we all looked the same.

THE BURNING OF SAN FRANCISCO

They were hunting ducks when the fog
swept down from the coastline and sent
the earth hissing out of existence:
picture embers doused by urine.
On they hunted through the white darkness,
singed branches and scrub
raking at their sides.

It is like wrapping your burnt tongue
inside someone else's;

so too did the fog take away the landscape,
the Transamerica tower,
the bridges, the problem of the homeless,
the ducks. When the air-raid sirens
sounded to guide them back
to the coastline, they could
not tell water from air. The sounds
faltered. So faint, the sounds,
faint as smoke, how do you

hear something in which you do not believe?
Did not this city in which they stand

burn down in 1906, is this second
obliteration little more than a demand
to recant all they have seen,
a seizure, a spurt in the brain,
saying: Recant.

THE MASTERLY PLAY OF FORM

When I show you a spot with
no fingerprint on my thumb,
I have already forgotten the knife
that veered off its line.
I only remember—nobody stopped
their work, none saw the
blood shine as webbing on water,
those people that talk through
their eyes, as if at Mass. For them,
work is throwing out the blade,
pulling the tang slowly back in
as one reels in rope, and though
I will always admire strength,
I would rather touch your wrists
as your strong hands break bread,
or know the wideness of the field
where we unshirted boys kicked
balls back and forth, amazed we
cleared such space in the grass,
men scattering outwards, all
with one stroke.

CONVALESCENCE

When you taste "sick,"
iron from lamb's blood,
sour mash filling your mouth,
you feel what your hands
feel after dropping something,
as on the first day
you reached for the table
to still yourself and found them
quaking like boiled water.

What you miss most is touching
the things in the other room,
and the color, of course,
the reason you moved back to
New York: fall leaves. The cardinals,
the brick walls you repaired.
The amaryllis flowers
and the sunset that are blossoming
black as we speak.

MINING EXPEDITION

We are looking for your glasses.
The pair you buried twenty years ago,
a thin strip of wire inside the ground.

There, by the marsh.
Was that where you caught crayfish,
or is it crawfish?
Was there always a cypress tree?

Some hikers pass us,
talking about violence in nature.
Eagle's prey
and fish that eat their own young.
Robin's eggs plummet

from the nest. The mantis bites off
her partner's head while mating.
Save your breath,

we know it already.
My friend the boxer has felt
fists in his stomach.

You see, I celebrate him,
I love the things man has made:
roasted food, terraces in the dirt.
The two hoops of gold that are
all you remember from growing up.

I walk in a path around nature
and find my way back, so do
hikers and miners, no

different from circumnavigating
a sanctuary, no different at all.

SALT

Last night a white pigeon flew through
the window and I scooped up every missile
I could find, a blouse, books, birds to kill
the bird that came despite rain and cold,
the same that watched at the sill while my
uncle hung himself at his hacienda, the
same that watched my grandmother bless
her sons then open her eyes in horror.
The nights after her death I dreamt of nothing
but the bird watching me as I made
love to my whitehaired professor, my body
rocking back and forth as if poised to leap
off a ledge, my skin growing slicker as
it watched. The room is still strewn with pages,
feathers, blues on the radio; this could be
wartime there is fear enough. So I take
cover while the rain laps the verandah
outside like a living thing in need of
attention and I bring a mattress for him
inside the forbidden room and lock
the doors in case the owners should return
and I close the shutters for spring is so cold
that the plants inside drop white flowers
onto the bed below. I am not listening;
I can barely hear him talk of the village

where he was born so overcome am I
by his child's eyes, he who believes the
flowers are for him, his arm unfolding
towards me like a key of flesh. At night
we lie awake in different beds. At night,
his thighs, luminous as salt from a mine.

THERE WERE NO HORSES

That summer,
no horses moving roughly
over the rocks, one incensed
at another, nudging its
head with a shout. We looked
for horses—you found some cars
but I only saw equine clouds
neighing silently at each other.
Ever since the dream of horses,
hundreds buried underground
like a crop of tomatoes
about to burst from the soil,
we wanted
not the clay horses of Xi'an,
no, though their hooves still tore
darkly through my mind like rainwater,
not the horses Xenophon says
were sent to the king of Persia
each one said to wear a bridle
of gold, but the real thing.
The stuff they feed to dogs.

THE RIVER

I

When we travel by boat, I am the one who always grows older, sometimes a beard appears, or my skin cracks and turns volcanic. But you stay the same, everything except your name, after a certain point you got up and said You can start calling me this from now on. After that there was always some confusion, are you Cecilia the girl I brought along to play Spanish guitar in the mornings, are you Natalie the woman that I have begun following after so many years?

II

It is true that you, Cecilia/Natalie, act differently: you've started eating the fish that we catch. No—there is no need, the fish here are small and bony, more like jewels than food. And your eyes shine yellow now at night, like a cat's. You once told me about a dream you had: floating in the salt water, face down, tasting fish as the schools swim past. No brassière. You've eaten so many fish you worry you'll sink, you worry you'll spend years at the bottom waiting for someone to find you, to kiss you, to cut open your stomach—only then will the rubies and sapphires tumble out and let you float again.

III

I thought about sapphires after that. I asked Were they blue? And you found a can of fish (always fish!) with a blue label and said Blue like this. But I shook my head, for that was just ink in the right hue, and even the whites of purity are created only by heating a black object until it glows. Your sapphires I knew as every eddy from aquamarine to Prussian to the not-blues, whites and reds, roiled together like an ocean. And I sat there swimming through the blue light while you waited on the deck and watched and smoked.

IV

Do you remember? You sitting barefoot like two pigeons pecking at the floorboards: it was how I found you when I first asked you to accompany me. And you shot back Are you running away from something? And I said No, it is the only way to stay untouched by the earth, and you wrinkled your nose and offered me tea, and thought for a moment and asked What happens if you run out of river? But that would be impossible, they used to believe in a huge river that encircled the earth, with a long serpent wound along the bottom. Just the same there is a never-ending river.

V

It was how I finally persuaded you to leave. Because
you saw the weeds growing up around you, deeper
than your shoulder, a dirty shade of green. You bristled
like a wet duck at the thought. No matter how con-
tent you looked with your TV dinners you still wor-
ried you might some day come down with scurvy.
And so your bags, your guitar, the river.

★

VI

In winter when there has been no sunlight for months
the water forgets its true color and begins to look the
same as the glass walls on the riverbanks. Cecilia ex-
plains: Sometimes a worker will spill white paint and
the whole river will brighten at the thought, so much
that he will want nothing more but to throw all his
paints in after the first, until the foreman notices his
look and curses him for it. To this place then people
come to watch the buildings take shape, sometimes on
the way to work, stepping out for a cup of coffee, and
there they will pass the afternoon, sitting on the quay
beneath towers and houses pinned as if to the lattice
of a spiderweb. And in the winter we sailed out of this
city, careful not to look down or listen to any of the
women sing as we passed.

VII

This is what they said to us in the port when we left:
We'll let you go, but please deliver these crates for
us. Their crates—I imagine silk clothes, coffee beans,
bottles of gin, also condoms, warnings, remonstrations,
old newspapers, unsifted pounds of mining roughage,
live snakes, philosophers' stones, burlap bags, and sev-
eral canisters of oenogarum & asafoetida. I have never
opened these crates, though you prodded them with
a crowbar and later I put my nose through the slats
of wood, eventually deciding they belonged to us as
much as anyone else, arranging some into a makeshift
bench and throwing some into the river.

VIII

But when you took the life of the boathand! A
boathand is not a crate to be so easily discarded, one
day I called for him and there you stood with a guilty
smile on your face, I don't even remember when we
hired the boathand, perhaps he was a stowaway, either
way he must have managed to swim ashore, I am cer-
tain of that. And it was just like you to take someone's
life, we are all capable of that, but how did you do it?
Did you push him overboard while he was singing
the cadenza of your favorite aria? Did you ask him to
swim out to find your hat that blew away in a gust of
wind? So I was upset about losing something I barely
knew I had.

IX

Still I was determined not to let that get in the way of our relations. There was too much to learn about navigation; it took up nearly all our time. The wind was always changing, so we had to adjust the controls, it was necessary to make sure the boat is turned the right way, by that I mean that sometimes the sky changed color so that the water was blue and the sky was green, or the water was gray and the sky was brown and the land was blue, it would have been no good to run the boat aground by accident. What you excelled at was guiding us onwards, for you were consumed with a passion to keep us going, you read the star-charts, you licked your finger to see which way the wind is moving, you even turned a stethoscope into a rudimentary astrolabe, which you held up to your eyes at night, squinting for hours.

X

And soon there was no need to navigate at all. When we sailed through the mangrove trees we quickly got lost in between their roots: one would point one way and another the opposite, it was a maze of arrows and signs. It even seemed they were moving faster than we were, certainly with more purpose, speaking louder than us, they had so much force, divine right or presence. When we walked we took care to use as few footsteps as possible; the sounds were of parrots squawking off in the distance, the sun like honey poured from a jar, so slow you could hear it shift across your feet, for a minute perched on your big toe like a golden scarab, and then inching up your leg. In this time we spoke to each other so majestically that it would take a week to finish a thought. Like this: Llllloooooooooooooooooooooooaaaaaaaaammmmmm. As I listened to a particularly long vowel I would close my eyes and steer in the warmest direction.

XI

As we were passing through the tropics you saw some fruit trees on the shore and begged me to bring you some fruit. Were you still worried about scurvy? This craving grew and grew until I saw how swollen your eyes had become thinking about it. And so I agreed and stripping off my clothes I waded through the warm water and felt the bottom break away. Soon came the pitch and tang of the mosquitoes, that wetness that followed me darkly for the next hour, and finally a soft fleshy newness of a leech pulling on my leg, twisting slightly: I felt two hooks working under my skin, a small thing, a sort of itch. Soon anything small enough became a leech, a forest and a colony of leeches, swollen with black blood, and when I pulled it away, one hook after the other, I felt what a snake feels after it has shed its skin and turns around to see what it has done. You said I, Cecilia, will not ask you to leave the boat again. But Natalie gave no such promise.

XII

The trees grew sparser and sparser and soon we saw a constellation of boats. Lights on everywhere to catch the squid, lights jutting out of the beams and oars and the people sitting by their nets, hands long ago deafened by coils of rope, and all throughout the night I heard what I thought were dogs barking in the distance, actually frogs with distended bellies, sitting by the shore and groaning loudly. It was about this time that you began to disturb my dreams, you becoming a strange woman who drills holes in the bottom of the boat. You argued it was to give the boat room to breathe, but then the river came alive, infuriated at this insult, sometimes in jets a white tumid river leaping upwards, and I could only wonder where we would all wash up.

XIII

Drill holes in our boat! You said Don't be ridiculous, I wouldn't do such a thing, but I held my tongue and there they sat, clusters of words smelling like overripe grapes. Black and sweet and engorged. But silent as I was mornings I felt sore enough to have been beaten in the night by men, perhaps several at once. And so I seethed and so the river boiled along with me. One day I threw a bowl of pears at the door and the whole boat heard the bowl clatter to the floor. It left a slick on the ground and even after you had cleaned it up the stain kept growing in our heads, shining wetly, the floorboards turned translucent. It was new ice over a lake; when we walked there the ground crazed and bore stretch marks: we both learned to walk around it.

XIV

That was the second time I left the boat. I only meant to catch some air, to dip my foot in the water, but instead each toe darted into the muck, anchored in position with such emotion as I had never seen on land. Now I knew the pride that piers feel to remain steadfast in the face of earthquakes, porpoises and other distractions. But by and by eucalyptus leaves and other residue floated past me, old newspapers and unsent letters declaiming absolute and irredeemable love, the roundness of the earth, also unpaid telephone bills, every line of which you read to me. It was as if you whispered that I was fated to kill my grandfather: suddenly I felt impatient, and wore my fate like a heavy coat against winter. And I tugged against my intransigent foot to go. The boulders I uprooted were massive and this weight carried us a ways downstream. During the tumult I heard you say to me:

Where will this end? Will it be that great salt sea on which men lie like children camped in a football field watching the sun blaze across the sky, these twin elements of salt and heat that work kilnlike to fire desires into a small, hard thing, a lump in the back of your throat, the Adam's apple of regret? And Natalie said Will it be that other silurian sea that has churned away all evidence like a man washing stains from clothes, kneading and dragging the cloth in his hands, into the same beige clay from which the best china is made, slender and bonewhite? And Natalie said Or will it just dry up, will children cross it ten times in an hour as they chase each other across this invisible line that I have drawn, a kite-string that bisects nothing, a river of great expectations that disappoints?

Notes & Acknowledgments

Telegonus, Agrius, Latinus: the three sons of Odysseus and Circe.

Refer to poem for citations in "Passage Interdit aux Non Musulmans" and "School of Dentistry."

For "There Were No Horses," refer to Xenophon, *Cyropaedia* 8.2.8.

"And About Time": title from the poem collected in David Lehman's *An Alternative to Speech*.

"A Season of Coal" is after Carmen Sisson, "Backstory: Home is Where the Fire Is." *Christian Science Monitor*, 9 August 2006.

"The Masterly Play of Form" is from Le Corbusier's definition of architecture, as published in *Towards a New Architecture*.

The River (II) is after Nin Andrews's "Adolescence," and *The River* (VII) contains part of Caelius Apicius's recipe for cooking truffles, from *De re coquinaria*.

My sincere thanks to John Cox, Kirk Lee Davis, Joann Kleinneiur, Rachel Nelson, and Carrie Strand Tebeau for their help with this book.

Grateful acknowledgement is made to the editors of the
following periodicals, in which these poems first appeared:

Ontario Review: "Balance"
The New Republic: "The Strike"
Ploughshares: "Potter's Fields"
Black Warrior Review: "Not That Our Empire Declines"
Harvard Review: "Instructions Received by New Colony"
Greensboro Review: "And About Time" (excerpt)
Prairie Schooner: "How to Care?" and "The Masterly Play
    of Form"
Heliotrope: "Salt" and "The River" (excerpt)
Michigan Quarterly Review: "Convalescence"
Cream City Review: "Passage Interdit aux Non Musulmans"
    and "The Burning of San Francisco"

green press

INITIATIVE

Ausable Press is committed to preserving ancient forests and natural resources. We elected to print *Mine* on 50% post consumer recycled paper, processed chlorine free. As a result, for this printing, we have saved:

2 Trees (40' tall and 6-8" diameter)
726 Gallons of Waste Water
292 Kilowatt Hours of Electricity
80 Pounds of Solid Waste
157 Pounds of Greenhouse Gases

Ausable Press made this paper choice because our printer, Thomson-Shore, Inc., is a member of Green Press Initiative, a nonprofit program dedicated to supporting authors, publishers, and suppliers in their efforts to reduce their use of fiber obtained from endangered forests.

For more information, visit www.greenpressinitiative.org